ANGR

Girls Dealing With Feelings

Gail Snyder

Copyright © 2015 by Enslow Publishers, Inc.

Jasmine Health, an imprint of Enslow Publishers, Inc.

All rights reserved.

No part of this book may be reproduced by any means without the written permission of the publisher.

Library of Congress Cataloging-in-Publication Data

Snyder, Gail.
  [Girls' guide to anger]
  Angry girl? : girls dealing with feelings / Gail Snyder.
    pages cm. — (Girls dealing with feelings)
  "Originally published in 2008 as the author's A girls' guide to anger.
  Includes bibliographical references and index.
    Summary: "Explores the emotion of anger in young women and the best ways to deal with it and the situations that cause it. Includes real-life examples, quotes, facts, tips, and quizzes"—Provided by publisher.
    ISBN 978-1-62293-030-2 — ISBN 978-1-62293-031-9 (pbk) — ISBN 978-1-62293-032-6 (ePUB) — ISBN 978-1-62293-033-3 (single-user PDF) — ISBN 978-1-62293-034-0 (multi-user PDF) 1. Anger.
  2. Girls—Life skills guides. I. Title.
  BF575.A5S63 2014
  155.5'33—dc23
                                      2013015764

Future editions:
Paperback ISBN: 978-1-62293-031-9
Single-User PDF ISBN: 978-1-62293-033-3

EPUB ISBN: 978-1-62293-032-6
Multi-User PDF ISBN: 978-1-62293-034-0

Printed in the United States of America
072014 HF Group, North Manchester, IN
10 9 8 7 6 5 4 3 2 1

To Our Readers: We have done our best to make sure all Internet addresses in this book were active and appropriate when we went to press. However, the author and the publisher have no control over and assume no liability for the material available on those Internet sites or on other Web sites they may link to. Any comments or suggestions can be sent by e-mail to comments@enslow.com or to the address below.

Jasmine Health
Box 398, 40 Industrial Road
Berkeley Heights, NJ 07922
USA
www.jasminehealth.com

Photo Credits: Shutterstock.com: Christos Georghiou (clipboard graphic), pp. 8, 44; Cory Thoman (brainstorm graphic), pp. 17, 54; freesoulproduction (thumbtack graphic), pp. 5, 6, 10, 16, 20, 32, 40, 41, 42, 46, 61, 62; NLshop (therapist graphic), pp. 11, 22, 24, 26, 27, 31, 33, 37, 49, 50, 51, 57, 60; Seamartini Graphics (atom graphic), pp. 9, 15; vectorgirl (lightbulb graphic), pp. 7, 23; zayats-and-zayats (quotation graphic), pp. 28, 38, 45, 48, 59.

Cover Photo: CREATISTA/Shutterstock.com

This book was originally published in 2008 as *A Girls' Guide to Anger*.

CONTENTS

1. I'm So Mad 4
2. How Do You Show Anger? 13
3. When Friends Make You Mad 19
4. Feeling Angry With Siblings 25
5. Keeping Your Cool With Adults 30
6. When You Keep Anger Inside 36
7. Mean Girls and Bullies 43
8. Don't Flip Out! 47
9. Resolving Conflicts 53
10. Using Your Anger 58

Find Out More 63
(Books, Internet Addresses, and Hotlines)

Index 64

CHAPTER ONE

I'm So Mad...

> *I couldn't believe it when my mother told me that I couldn't go to Kelsey's party. I had been looking forward to it for weeks. Mom told me I had stay home just because I had gotten another bad report card. I tried to tell her how unfair it was, but she wouldn't listen to me.*
>
> *I ran upstairs to my room and slammed the door so hard it cracked. Then I scooped up a sculpture of a dog I made that my mother really liked and hurled it to the floor. It broke into a million satisfying pieces. I was standing in the middle of the room with my heart pounding and my hands curled into fists. All I could think was, what else could I throw?*
>
> —Jenna

Jenna was experiencing all of the physical symptoms of having kicked into anger mode. Her heart was racing, her body was stiff, and she couldn't think clearly.

Whenever you are angry, your body automatically reacts the same way, regardless of the situation. Your muscles get tense and your heart starts to beat faster.

These changes in your body mean you are physically ready to respond to the threat before you.

This response is known as the "fight-or-flight" instinct. It has been part of being human since prehistoric times, when people needed to deal with wild animals and other dangers. The instinct allows the body to prepare to stand and confront a threat or to run away.

This fight-or-flight instinct is an automatic response that helps protect you from harm. But it also occurs when there isn't any actual physical danger—only the feeling of needing to protect yourself from some kind of threat or danger. The same response happens whether a speeding car is hurtling toward you, or you hear a particularly nasty insult from a boy you

Fight-or-Flight Emotions

The fight-or-flight instinct typically involves the basic emotions of both fear and anger. Anger (like any other emotion) rarely exists for very long before another emotion or two come into play. If you can identify the pattern of emotions you are feeling, you are on your way to being able to take charge of them.

I'm So Mad . . .

You and Your Emotions

A part of everyone's personality, emotions are a powerful driving force in life. They are hard to define and understand. But what is known is that emotions—which include anger, fear, love, joy, jealousy, and hate—are a normal part of the human system. They are responses to situations and events that trigger bodily changes, motivating you to take some kind of action.

Some studies show that the brain relies more on emotions than on intellect in learning and in making decisions. Being able to identify and understand the emotions in yourself and in others can help you in your relationships with family, friends, and others throughout your life.

What Happens When You're Angry?

1. dilated pupils
2. tears
3. feeling flushed
4. dry mouth
5. a knot in the stomach
6. rapid breathing

> The word *anger* describes emotions that cover a wide range. When you are angry, you may be mildly annoyed, somewhat irritated, rather mad, simply outraged, or incredibly furious.

can't stand. This protective instinct causes your body to respond whenever you feel irritated, disrespected, shamed, or embarrassed by others.

Lots of things can make you angry. Sometimes the unfairness of events in your life may seem overwhelming. It may be that one of your friends kissed the boy you've had a crush on, or a girl is spreading rumors about you at school. Or perhaps you believe that your parents are being unfair because they give your brother more freedom than you have. In all of these cases, you can experience various emotions, along with anger.

You may be having a lot of trouble dealing with your emotions these days. This is especially true if you are going through the physical changes of puberty—the stage when your body is maturing into that of an adult. Controlling your emotions during puberty can be especially hard. That's because the emotional center of the brain—the amygdala—is in charge. As you grow older, the part of the brain that handles

> ### The Survey Says...
>
> In a national poll, Harvard University researchers surveyed more than 1,500 middle and high school students about their anger. One third admitted that they had trouble controlling their anger. Twenty-one percent of the girls said they had gotten into fights because they had been insulted, disrespected, or involved in an ongoing disagreement. More than twice the number of boys made the same admission.

reasoning and judgment—the prefrontal cortex—will be in control. So while the amygdala is running the show, you can experience emotional highs and lows that make you feel like you're out of control. During this time in your life, even little things may set you off and make you feel mad.

Your changing moods are also affected by special chemical substances in your body called hormones. During puberty, the levels of hormones in a girl's body, especially estrogen and progesterone, keep changing. These hormones affect behavior and mood. So when the levels of hormones in your body keep changing, your moods can change, too. You are also more likely to get angry because nobody seems to understand you.

Just feeling sad or stressed out can make you grouchy and angry over things that may not normally bother you at all. For example, if your life is going smoothly, a bad grade on your math test may upset you a little, but you'll just resolve to study harder next time. However, if that same test result happens after you've been grounded for staying out too late, you are likely to get angry and upset. If you are tired or not feeling well, you may also be more likely to take offense or get angry.

How you express your anger. How do you act when you're angry? Some people physically and verbally lash out. They yell at or hit others, break things, or act mean. They're expressing anger by being aggressive—that is, by acting in hostile or violent

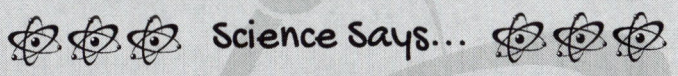

Science Says...

When you are angry, a hormone known as adrenaline is released into the bloodstream. The high amount of adrenaline energizes you and causes blood to rush through your body. That's why your face turns red and your heart beats faster when you have angry feelings. Adrenaline can fuel a rush that takes over, making you feel overwhelmed, powerless, and out of control.

Expressing Anger

There are big differences in the way girls and boys express anger, says author Rachel Simmons in *Odd Girl Speaks Out: Girls Write About Bullies, Cliques, Popularity, and Jealousy* (2004). American society tends to expect boys to directly show anger—with words or physically, although only if they don't seriously hurt anyone. However, girls are often taught that expressing their anger this way is bad.

As a result, if a girlfriend is angry at you, it is likely that she won't come out and tell you so. You may have to figure it out by the clues she leaves. She may tease you about something she's never brought up before, stop talking to you, or tell stories about you that aren't true. But what she may not do is tell you what made her angry or give you a chance to make it up to her.

ways. Being aggressive with others seldom solves any issues. In fact, it often leads to more problems because it makes the person on the receiving end angry, too.

However, it is possible to express your anger in ways that don't harm others. You are taking charge of your anger when you communicate your feelings in healthy ways—that is, by being honest and up-front but not hurtful. This way of talking with friends, parents, teachers, and other people in your life can help you improve your relationships with them.

For example, Elise and Jamie have been friends for a long time. But Jamie has a habit that has been getting on Elise's nerves. Whenever Elise asks Jamie for her opinion, Jamie doesn't give one. She usually replies, "I don't care—whatever you want." Jamie's laid-back attitude had really been bothering Elise lately, and she finally decided to say something about it. Although she was feeling angry, she spoke calmly as she explained her frustration with Jamie. Although Jamie felt surprised at first, she appreciated her friend's honesty, and she promised to make some changes. Both girls felt better about their friendship.

Getting a grip on your anger is important. Are you quick to anger? Do you break things when you get mad? Have you ever hurt anyone when you were angry? Did you feel bad about it afterward? Do you believe you are having trouble dealing with people

When you get angry, you have choices: you can choose to stay angry or you can calm down and think about how to resolve your issues.

because you can't manage angry feelings? If you answered yes to any of these questions, then you need some help dealing with your anger and learning better ways to express your feelings.

Just remember, feeling angry is normal. It is the actions you take as a result of your anger that can solve conflicts and problems, or make them worse. Anger can be a real problem in your life if you let it. But learning to manage your anger will not only improve your relationships with others, but also help make you feel better about yourself. By practicing some of the ideas and tips in this book, you will understand this powerful emotion and have the tools to handle anger in yourself as well as in others.

CHAPTER TWO

How Do You Show Anger?

> One day at school, Angela and Erica were talking between classes. Suddenly, Felice burst in on their conversation. Shoving Erica hard against the lockers, Felice angrily accused the younger girl of flirting with her boyfriend. Angela knew Felice was just being a bully and that the claim wasn't true. So she was shocked to hear Erica quickly apologize and say it wouldn't happen again. Angela was angry for her friend. She turned to Felice and in a cool, firm voice told her to leave Erica alone.

Different people will often react to the same incident in different ways. One person step backs and claims not to be bothered, another person is inspired to take some kind of action, and a third person becomes furious. Are you like that third person? Do you tend to get angry often? Take the quizzes on pages 17 and 54 to find out.

Your answers to the quiz may depend on your personality. In general, if you have an aggressive personality, you tend to get angry easily—and show that anger—more often than people who are assertive or passive. So what exactly are these different kinds of personalities?

Aggressive. People who have aggressive personalities usually don't give much thought to other people's feelings because they typically put their needs ahead of anyone else's. They often seem to think they know best and are better than other people. When something goes wrong, they find someone else to blame rather than themselves. Quick to anger, aggressive personalities often number among the bullies at school. They're also the people most likely to get sent to the principal's office for talking back to teachers or getting into fights. Using threats to get what they want, aggressive people are often feared by their classmates but are typically not well liked or admired.

Passive. People with passive personalities tend to fear confrontations. When faced with a situation that would make most people mad, they often don't look angry. There is no red face, clenched fists, or heavy breathing. Because they simply want the uncomfortable situation to go away, they deal with it—and most confrontations—by giving in. They

> ### ✦✦✦ Science Says... ✦✦✦
>
> James Averill, author of the book *Anger and Aggression* (1982), says most people experience anger several times a week. Some people become angry several times each day. Yet Averill's research shows that only 10 percent of the time does this anger result in someone physically hurting another person. In fact, he found that 19 percent of the time the angry persons funneled their emotions into being "extra nice." In other words, they behaved in a passive way, by not directly dealing with the situation by standing up for themselves.

will assume blame for a problem, even when they are innocent, and often place other people's needs ahead of their own. They don't attempt to seek revenge, but they don't try to suggest a fair and proper solution to the problem either. Some passive people act that way because they don't value themselves—they suffer from low self-esteem.

Assertive. People with assertive personalities try to understand and support everyone's rights. Because they tend to have high self-esteem, they believe other people are not necessarily out to hurt or take advantage of them. Their high self-esteem means they can listen to criticism and consider its merits. They respond to disagreements without taking offense or thinking they are stupid or worthless. When an assertive person is faced with a situation that could cause anger, he or she thinks about the best way to resolve the problem before acting.

A complex combination. Of course, it is possible that you can see yourself in some of the descriptions of each of these personality types. Most people don't fall neatly into a single category. Depending on the situation and the people involved, you may act in a different way. For instance, at home you might demonstrate passive behavior with your parents, while at school, you may be assertive with your classmates and friends.

However, you will find that in most cases, when you act assertive, you will have the best results in dealing with others. When you are assertive, you are

Anger as a Way of Life?

People who anger easily often have a set pattern of beliefs, attitudes, and expectations of themselves and of others. They often believe that their way is the only way to do things, and they feel threatened when others question their actions.

Rate Yourself: Do You Get Angry Easily?

Do you agree with the following statements? Give yourself three points if your answer is "often," two points if it is "some of the time," one point if "rarely," and zero points for "never."

1. If my friend cancels on me at the last minute, I get mad at her.
2. I hate waiting in line.
3. When someone disagrees with me, I make sure they know they are wrong.
4. When I get mad, I throw, hit, or break things.
5. I get angry at myself when I do something wrong or badly.
6. When someone treats me poorly, I think about ways that I can get back at them.
7. I've gotten in trouble at school because of my anger.
8. I have been so angry that I have pushed, kicked, or slapped another person.
9. Other people have told me that I get angry too much or that I am scary when I get mad.
10. I curse at people when I get mad and try to make them feel bad.
11. Sometimes I don't feel like I'm in control of my anger.
12. I am easily offended by comments people make about me and can't stop thinking about them.
13. I frequently feel bad about things I have said or done while I was mad.
14. When I dislike someone, I let them know.
15. When I don't get my way, I get very upset.

***Add up the numbers: 0–8 points** means you're pretty good at handling situations that make people angry. Anger sometimes causes problems in your life if your score is **9–20**. More than **20 points** indicates that you probably get angry easily—and that you need to find better ways to handle your anger.*

Adapted from David J. Decker and Mike Obsatz, "Your Anger Index: How Angry and Hostile Are You?" ANGEResources.com able to honestly communicate your feelings. Although that doesn't guarantee you will always get what you want, you will feel better when you can honestly share things with friends, family members, and other important people in your life. And by talking about your emotions, you will prevent them from staying bottled up inside of you—which can cause even more problems. By being assertive, you will let others know how they can better consider your feelings in the future.

Learned behaviors. Your temperament and personality aren't the only influences on how you experience and express feelings of anger—and other emotions for that matter. Over the years, you may have learned certain ways of dealing with anger based on how your parents or friends behaved in stressful situations. If your parents yelled and hollered when they were angry, it's likely you do the same thing, too. Some scientists report that teens who respond with violence when they are angry do so because they were exposed to it while growing up—either by witnessing it or being the victims of it. Even if you've learned some unhealthy ways of expressing anger, you can unlearn those behaviors.

CHAPTER THREE

When Friends Make You Mad

> Kaitlyn sat on the step of her porch, stewing over what just happened. Mackenzie had actually broken up her party by inviting everyone over to her house. "We'll be back in an hour or so," she said. "But you should probably hang around until your other guests come." It was now three hours later, and no one else had arrived. Maybe they were at Mackenzie's house, too. Kaitlyn was furious at her so-called friend and wondered why she had invited her in the first place.

You can have the best time of your life when with friends. They can make you feel understood, respected, and a part of something. But you can be devastated by friends, too, when they disappoint you, hurt your feelings, or make you angry.

There are many ways that friends can upset you. You may be angry over something a girlfriend said or did. Or you can be disappointed to learn she didn't tell you the truth. Perhaps your team lost the big

Five Major Conflict Starters Between Friends

1. Boys
2. Gossip
3. Feeling left out
4. Betrayed trust
5. Lies and mean comments

game, and you think one of your teammates didn't make her best effort. Or you're upset that your party was a bust because one the girls you invited was rude, and your friends went home early. Maybe one of your friends got caught talking in class, and the teacher decided to keep everyone after school.

Researchers have found that when girls are angry, they tend not to be honest with each other. They are hesitant to confront one another and say what they are feeling. Instead, they often stop talking altogether and give each other the silent treatment. If girls would talk frankly with each other, professor of psychology Sharon Lamb says, they would probably find ways to resolve their differences. "In all relationships, if you get angry with people, you talk it out," she says.

Talk to each other. If you want to keep your friendship, there are steps you can take to mend an argument:

- Make the first move. Don't let your anger grow. By taking the first step, you're showing your friend how important your friendship is to you. At this point, you don't need to apologize or admit fault. Make it clear that you want to talk.
- Be prepared about what you want to say. Think about the points you want to make. It may help to write them down ahead of time.
- Be prepared to listen. At the beginning of your conversation, establish a rule that neither of you is to interrupt the other. Then, be sure to listen—don't think about what you're going to say next. Pay attention to what your friend is saying.
- Try to empathize with your friend. That is, try to see and understand her point of view.

Accept responsibility if you are at fault. If you discover that you have wronged the other person, sincerely apologize for what you have done. If you receive an apology from the other person, graciously accept it and do your best to forgive her and put the incident behind you.

A True Apology Should Be Given
1. With sincerity
2. With a genuine understanding of the issue
3. Without any conditions
4. Without the expectation of an apology in return

When speaking with the other person, it helps to use statements that begin with the word *I* and not the word *you*. I-messages allow you to clearly state your feelings. In a calm voice, state what is bothering you, why it bothers you, and what you think ought to be done about it. Don't expect anyone to know what you are thinking unless you tell him or her.

When a friend is angry with you. There may be times when a friend acts angry with you for no clear reason. Before you get angry in return, stop and consider what might be making him or her irritable. Do you sometimes find yourself in a negative mood, when nothing seems to be going right? Maybe your friend is not acting like him- or herself for the same reason. Recognize that if a friend is saying or doing negative things, it may be because he or she is feeling bad about something. Rather than take harsh words too personally, give your friend a day or two. Then see if he or she wants to talk. By trying to understand what's going on in your friend's heart and mind, you don't make the situation worse by yelling or retaliating in some other way.

When dealing with angry confrontations, do your best to keep lines of communication open. Rather than expressing your anger by giving your friend the silent treatment, keep talking until you find a solution to your problem.

Use "I," Not "You"

I-messages allow you to tell someone how you feel without placing blame on the person involved in a conflict. I-messages focus on how the problem affects you and what you would like to see happen to fix things. It has four basic parts:

1. "I feel…" (States the emotions you are feeling.)
2. "…when…" (Gives details about what the other person did or said that caused the hard feelings.)
3. "…because…" (Explains why you feel that way. This can be the hardest part of the I-message.)
4. "I want…" (Describes what you think will resolve the conflict or ease the bad feelings.)

When a Friend Is Angry

1. **Stay upbeat and positive.** Don't say anything to make the person angrier. Let your friend have his or her say without interrupting.

2. **Know when to back off.** If your friend needs time to cool down, give him or her some space. Be sure you have a conversation later, when he or she is ready to talk calmly.

3. **If you think your friend's anger is justified, show some empathy.** When he or she is ready to talk, discuss ways to deal with the issue and manage that anger.

4. **Steer him or her away from destructive behavior.** Let your friend know you will stop him or her from harming others or himself or herself. Talk to a parent or teacher if you are concerned that your friend might engage in destructive behavior.

CHAPTER FOUR

Feeling Angry With Siblings

> Eleven-year-old Allison is four years younger than her sister Amber. When their parents go out, Amber is often asked to babysit Allison. But Allison hates it when her older sister is in charge. Amber orders her around and curses at her and calls her names as soon as their parents leave the house.

If you have a sister and you seem to always be fighting with her, you are not alone. Most sisters—and brothers—are often at odds. But conflicts can become serious problems when kids express anger with verbal abuse or physical violence. There are several different ways that Allison can respond to her sister's aggressive behavior. Which do you think will have the best results?

Don't say anything at all. This passive approach will do nothing to stop Amber's behavior. In addition, if Amber continues to treat her younger sister this way,

Skills Needed to Work Out Solutions

1. Being respectful
2. Being understanding
3. Being assertive

the relationship between the two of them will remain hostile. In addition, by holding her feelings in, Allison runs the risk of reaching a breaking point and reacting with violence. This is definitely not a good solution.

Yell and scream back at Amber. Although Allison may think she feels better by venting, she is making a bad situation worse. Name-calling and harsh words tend to make the other person in a conflict even angrier than she was before. And again, it can lead to violence.

Walk away from the situation at first and wait until she feels calmer. When Allison's over her stormy feelings, she should try to have a conversation with Amber to see if there is a specific issue that sets off her sister's anger. It is important that she confront Amber, saying something like, "We need to talk this through." She needs to be assertive—to stand her ground and

> Feeling angry—no matter what the cause—is never an excuse for violence or abuse.

tell Amber to stop. If this last approach doesn't work, Allison needs to bring her parents into the picture. They should know what's going on.

Conflicts among sisters and brothers are normal. Family members bicker and have arguments with one another for the same reasons they argue with other people. Both want the other person to see things from his or her own point of view.

Many siblings fight because of jealousy. A sister may become very angry if she believes her parents are playing favorites. Or a girl may complain that her parents are not being fair because she and her brother have to abide by different family rules and curfews. Relationships among brothers and sisters are usually most strained when siblings are of the same gender and near one another in age.

Conflicts between siblings also occur when they don't respect each other's property. For instance, suppose you are angry with your sister because she

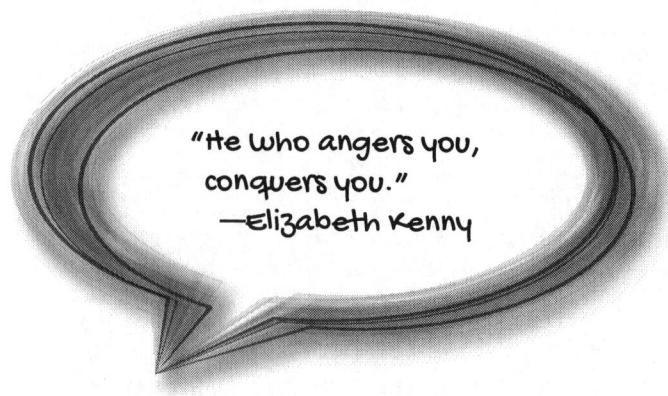

"He who angers you, conquers you."
—Elizabeth Kenny

wore your favorite jeans without your permission. To make matters worse, when she was done with them, she dropped them inside out on the floor of her room. You could complain loudly, "You always borrow my stuff without asking me and never return it to its proper place!" However, you-statements with words like "always" and "never" are likely to make your sister defensive. She'll probably hurl an accusation of her own right back at you.

Manage your conflicts. If you really want to solve the conflict and prevent it from happening again, you need to use some conflict management techniques. Your sister will be less inclined to take offense if you use an I-message to explain why you're angry: "I'm upset because you borrowed my jeans without asking me. They are my favorite pair, and I saved a long time before I was able to buy them." Be sure to follow up with a sentence explaining how you'd like things to go in the future: "Next time, please ask my permission before you go in my closet."

Know when to ask for help. Sometimes hard feelings can't be resolved on your own. If you have tried to work things out with your sister without success, or if you and your brother keep fighting, you need to talk to your parents. When you tell your side of the story, try to keep your voice calm and use I-messages to describe your feelings. Don't attack your sibling with words or fists. It is important that your parents understand your feelings of anger. And they will be impressed to see that you know how to manage conflict in the family in a mature way.

CHAPTER FIVE

Keeping Your Cool With Adults

> Lindsey loved basketball. However, she knew that her parents didn't approve of girls playing sports. Although she wanted to try out for the basketball team in seventh grade, Lindsey did not dare oppose her parent's wishes. Instead, she joined the debate club because it was an activity that her mother and father thought to be more suitable for a girl.
>
> Lindsey didn't tell her parents about how much she wanted to play basketball. But she felt angry at them for refusing to allow her to go out for the team. That anger did not go away. Instead, it resurfaced every time she argued with her parents about other things.

Lindsey was angry with her parents but didn't know how to express her feelings. All she knew was that her parents didn't understand what was important to her. And she didn't feel like she could talk to them or change their way of thinking.

Part of growing up involves breaking away from your parents, as you begin to want to think for yourself

Anger in the Family

Every family is different in the way its members handle anger. Kids often learn from what they experience at home. If your mom and dad yell at you a lot or even at each other, you are likely to express your anger in the same manner.

However, be aware that this method of dealing with your anger isn't likely to produce good results. It is important to remember that you have a choice on how you respond when you are angry. It is up to you to decide how you will act—being aggressive or being calm and assertive.

---

and make your own decisions. From time to time, you will probably get angry when you have differences of opinion with your mother, father, or other adult family members. If you are upset about a parental rule that you think is unfair or babyish, you need to let your mother and father know how you feel.

However, the way that you express your opinion is important. Yelling, breaking things, or storming off to your room won't get you very far. A more effective solution would be to wait until you are no longer upset. Then, approach your parents and in a quiet voice ask to talk further. During your discussion, stay calm and use logical arguments to explain your side.

Family stresses. The same holds true when you're angry about other issues. Family changes and other stresses such as divorce, unemployment, money problems, abuse, illness, or impending moves can increase feelings of anger and tension in households. The best way to deal with your feelings is to try to talk with the adults in your life about how you are affected by what's going on. If you express your anger by refusing to talk to others, you won't change anything. And you won't feel very good about yourself, either.

If your parents are angry with you, try to step back from arguing with them. Stop and think about where your parents may be coming from. They may be having

Teens Say Their Parents Make Them Angry...

1. "When I have a lot of things on my mind that I can't do anything about and then my parents ask me to do something when I'm already tired and overloaded."
2. "When there are other priorities, no time for me, and I feel like I don't matter."
3. "When my parents are unfair and there's no point in talking to them."

Quoted in Michael G. Conner, "Why Do Teenagers Get So Angry?" *Family News*, 2003

Tips on Talking to Parents and Other Adults

1. **Bring up your issue when the adult has the time to listen.** Don't try to talk to your parents when they're busy with something or someone else or rushing out the door. Say, "Is this a good time for you? I have something important to discuss."

2. **Be aware of your body language.** Don't roll your eyes, cross your arms, or clench your fists. Look the other person in the eyes and try to remain calm.

3. **Use respectful language.** Don't use sarcasm, insults, or put-downs when explaining your point of view. Snapping something like, "That's a stupid reason," will only make the other person angrier.

4. **Be honest.** Tell the truth about how you feel or what has happened; your parents and other adults want to trust you.

5. **Listen to the other side of the issue.** The adult will be more likely to show you the same respect.

6. **State your case using I-messages.** "I feel pressured because I need to get this report done tonight, so I don't really have time to walk the dog," or "I don't agree because..."

a hard time with work, with an ill family member, or some other stressful situation. As a result, they may not be thinking clearly. They may even be taking their anger out on you.

In dealing with an angry parent, don't try to explain your side of the story right away. Instead, wait for a while until your mom or dad has calmed down. Then, in a respectful voice, use an I-message to explain where you are coming from. If you feel your mother or father is unable to connect with you, you may want to talk to another trusted adult or to a school counselor.

Dealing with other adults. Your parents probably aren't the only adults who may make you angry sometimes. For example, you may believe that some of your teachers are treating you unfairly, or letting some students in your class get away with breaking rules while coming down hard on you. In some cases, you may also believe that teachers are favoring certain students over others.

Some students complain that their teachers get mad and yell too much at their students, sometimes singling out a kid in front of the whole class. Rather than simply complaining among themselves about a teacher's actions, students might feel better if they made the effort to point out the problem. After all, it is possible that a teacher is not aware she's upset a student who thinks she's picking on him or that her kids think she is playing favorites.

If you are angry with your teacher, don't try to talk in the heat of your anger. Take some time to settle down and think about what you can do. If you think you can discuss your problem calmly, you should try to have a conversation with your teacher so you can let him or her know your problem. Be courteous and polite. Don't confront the teacher and put him or her on the defensive by making wild accusations.

If you are not happy with the outcome, you should take your concerns home with you and share them with your parents. Tell them what's been happening in class and answer any questions they may have. Simply taking this step may actually help you feel better right away, especially if your parents are sympathetic to your story. Their next step may be to go to school and have a meeting with your teacher and school administrator. In most cases, a parent-teacher meeting will make things better for everyone.

If you are afraid to talk to your parents about your problem, you can approach your school guidance counselor instead. Talking things out with another adult can help you focus on exactly what is going on in your head and in the teacher's. You may discover options you had not thought about.

CHAPTER SIX

When You Keep Anger Inside

> Carol was having terrible headaches and stomachaches. Her worried mother took her to the doctor, who was unable to find a medical cause for the symptoms. He then referred Carol and her mother to a therapist—someone who treats people with relationship problems. After working with the family therapist for a while, Carol finally opened up to him. She mentioned that her mother had just begun a job with evening hours. Carol's headaches and stomachaches always occurred on school nights, when she was home alone.

Carol was angry about a lot of things, but she couldn't express her anger. Her parents had just divorced, and she was angry about the breakup. She had moved to a new school and was angry about losing her best friend. And she was angry that her mother's new job hours meant Carol was left alone in the evening. However, Carol didn't acknowledge any of that anger. She figured her mother had enough on

It's Hard to Ignore Anger

Anger is like an inflatable beach ball that you can't really push completely underwater. It keeps popping back up at you, no matter how hard you try to keep it down. In the same way, no matter how hard you try to keep anger inside, or force it down, it will come back up.

So don't try to hide your anger. You'll only end up staying angry for a much longer time than you would have if you had acknowledged it. You need to express your angry feelings, although not with hostile actions or words. Talk it out with a friend, parent, or other trusted person. You'll find that your anger will go away a lot more quickly that way than if you keep it hidden.

---

her plate trying to support the family that she didn't need to hear about Carol's problems.

In fact, when her mother had asked Carol if she minded the late-night work hours, Carol hadn't been able to explain how she felt. Although the new work hours really did bother Carol, she kept her feelings to herself. And her suppressed anger surfaced in the form of headaches and stomachaches.

The mind's effect on the body. When you suppress your emotions, you can make yourself physically ill. Holding in anger causes many different

When You Keep Anger Inside

problems, including dizziness, teeth grinding, and tense, aching muscles. Suppressed anger can also make you sick with an ulcer, a stomachache, or a headache.

In Carol's case, she began to feel better after working for a while with a family therapist. He helped Carol talk about her troubles and learn skills to help her deal with her new situation.

Low self-esteem. Sometimes, kids who are feeling overwhelmed by stressful situations direct their anger inward. This typically occurs with people who have low self-esteem. They become angry with themselves, often putting themselves down and discouraging themselves with thoughts like "I'm really a loser" or "I can't do anything right." Their low self-esteem makes it hard for them to deal with everyday stresses of life or to believe other people could possibly like them.

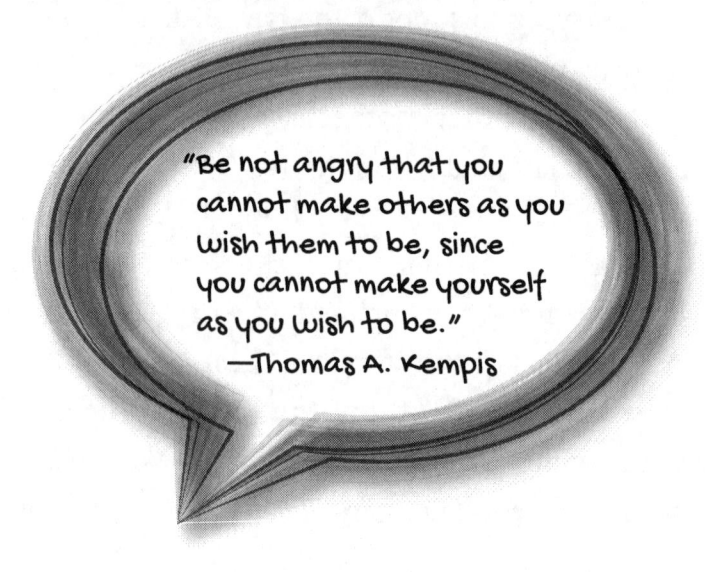

> "Be not angry that you cannot make others as you wish them to be, since you cannot make yourself as you wish to be."
> —Thomas A. Kempis

Self-esteem issues can develop at any time. Some girls struggle with their feelings when the family goes through a divorce. Others become unhappy with the way their bodies change during puberty or obsess over their weight, believing they are too fat or too thin. Perfectionists who have high expectations for themselves become angry when they don't meet their goals. When low self-esteem issues combine with difficulty expressing anger and other emotional problems, serious eating disorders can result.

Eating disorders. One of the most serious disorders linked with anger and low self-esteem issues is anorexia nervosa. The disorder, in which a person has an obsessive desire to lose weight, affects mostly girls. In an effort to control something in life, a girl with anorexia nervosa severely restricts the amount of food she eats and constantly exercises to keep the pounds off. But no matter how much weight she loses, she believes she needs to lose more.

A similar eating disorder is bulimia, which involves the desire for extreme weight loss. However, the bulimic person overeats and then makes herself throw up the consumed food so she won't gain any weight.

Both of these eating disorders can result in life-threatening weight loss because their victims don't get enough nutrients from food. But without proper medical treatment, the victims of these emotional disorders don't recognize that they are in danger of killing themselves.

Overeating has also been linked to teens with problems dealing with anger. A professor of behavioral science at the University of Texas Health Science Center, William Mueller, headed a study that found that teens who had trouble expressing anger were likely to have eating disorders and an unhealthy increase in weight. "They tend to isolate themselves, watch TV or read rather than connecting with their friends," he noted in the study.

Depression. Girls with low self-esteem and suppressed anger are also at risk for developing clinical depression. Its symptoms include feelings of sadness, hopelessness, and fatigue that last over a long period of time—weeks, months, or longer. People diagnosed

> Anorexia usually develops in girls who are ages 12–25 years old. Most victims of this disorder are perfectionists who do not cope well with change, including the natural changes that occur when their bodies undergo puberty.

> Depression typically affects kids who are experiencing stressful situations, such as a chronic illness or the death of family members. Others may have undergone traumatic experiences, such as physical or sexual abuse or a natural disaster.

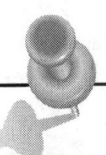

with depression will withdraw from activities with friends, family, and others. They may stop doing schoolwork or going to school.

Depression interferes with a person's ability to socialize with other people. Major depressive disorder affects an estimated 5 percent of teens in the United States. Severe depression can distort thinking and lead to self-destructive behavior such as drug and alcohol abuse. Severely depressed individuals may hurt themselves by cutting or even try to kill themselves. If not treated, clinical depression can lead to suicide, which is the third leading cause of death among fifteen- to twenty-five-year-olds.

Get help. If you believe that you or a friend may be suffering from clinical depression, don't ignore your feelings. It is very important that you do something to get help for anyone who shows signs of depression. Talk to a trusted friend or your parents, school counselor,

Some Symptoms of Depression

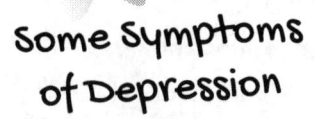

1. Loss of interest in favorite activities or hobbies
2. Ongoing feelings of sadness and hopelessness
3. Easily irritated and angered
4. Feelings of worthlessness or guilt
5. Low energy
6. Stomachaches and headaches
7. Difficulty relating to people socially
8. Changes in eating or sleeping habits
9. Trouble concentrating or following a conversation

religious leader, or other adult. If you are not sure who can help, you can call the suicide prevention hotline shown on page 63.

When other people know what's going on in your or your friend's life, they will be able to help. Disorders such as anorexia nervosa, bulimia, and clinical depression are treatable. With medication and therapy, as well as support from family and friends, it is possible for victims of these disorders to overcome them.

CHAPTER SEVEN

Mean Girls and Bullies

> When Kathy entered the seventh grade, she suddenly became a social outcast. She had no one to eat lunch with and was never invited to parties. The other girls teased her about her glasses, her body, and the way she dressed. "There was a lot of plotting and scheming behind people's backs. It was horrible," she later recalled. "I don't remember anything I learned that year."
>
> Quoted in Nanci Hellmich, "Caught in the Catty Corner," *USA Today*, April 9, 2002

Kathy's treatment by the other girls in her school is called "relational aggression." The term refers to a nonphysical form of bullying in which relationships are used to harm another person. When guys want to hurt other guys, they usually do so with their fists. But when girls want to hurt other girls, they are more likely to use words. They spread rumors and gossip, pass notes, talk about the outcast behind her back, and find other ways to be cruel.

Girls who are bullies use their power to abuse others. Their victims may not suffer from physical pain, but they do suffer emotionally from the bullying. According to the National Association of School Psychologists, each day more than 160,000 children refuse to go to school because they know that one or more bullies are waiting for them. Being teased or physically threatened by peers saps the victim's self-esteem and makes her feel helpless to stop the attacks.

Use anger to stand up for yourself. If a girl is being constantly teased by bullies, says psychologist Sharon Lamb, she can use her anger to stand up for herself. If she doesn't, then she will go on being victimized. The girl should respond to her tormentor by asserting

Cyberbullying Is a Serious Problem

A 2004 survey by i-Safe America of 1,500 fourth through eighth graders reported:

42 percent of them had been bullied online

35 percent had been threatened online

53 percent said hurtful things to others online

58 percent did not tell their parents or any other adult about being bullied.

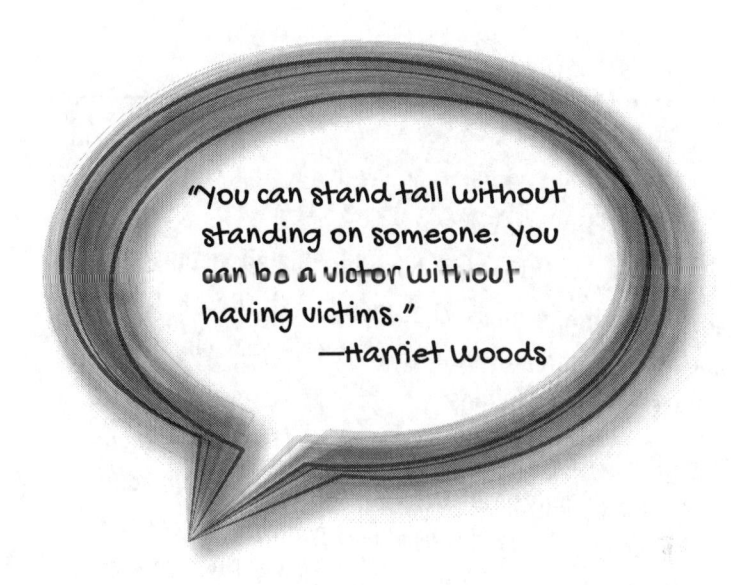

> "You can stand tall without standing on someone. You can be a victor without having victims."
> —Harriet Woods

herself, saying something like, "What you are doing is hurtful, and there is no good reason to treat me this way." When confronting a bully, she should also try to hide her anger. Bullies feed off of the reactions they get from their victims. If the person doesn't react, they are likely to find someone else to target.

When Kathy was having trouble with bullies at school, she found her parents always willing to listen. She could talk about how she was hurting and appreciated their concern.

According to Kathy, she learned a lot about her experience and now tries to treat everyone she knows with respect. She said, "I catch myself when I want to say something mean, and I stop because I know what it feels like to be on the other side."

Bullying on the Web

In recent years, "cyberbullies" have humiliated victims using instant messaging, e-mails, chat rooms, Web sites, and blogs to gossip and spread rumors. A twelve-year-old student from Massachusetts explains:

> "It gets pretty ugly in terms of how [girls] treat each other. They spread rumors that aren't necessarily true. It basically has to do with being jealous of how popular someone is. I think it's just as harmful as physical violence. The difference is this is a little less likely to be seen by teachers. You can just break up a fight. This is a lot more complicated."

Quoted in Gail Spector, "Author to Speak on Ways to Deal With Girl Bullies," *Boston Globe*, December 15, 2002

If you or someone you know is being bullied at school, you need to get help. Even though you may find it hard to do, talk to an adult—your parents, a teacher, or the principal. Schools take bullying seriously and have a plan in place for dealing with it. Although it can be difficult to get involved, if you witness someone else being bullied, don't stand by silently. Stand up for the victim if you can. However, if you feel as though you will place yourself in a dangerous position by doing so, report the incident to a teacher as soon as possible.

CHAPTER EIGHT

Don't Flip Out!

> As Lydia was walking down the hall, two girls—Alisha and Bianca—bumped into her. Alisha gave a short laugh and continued walking, but Bianca stopped. She glared at Lydia in mock indignation and asked, "Why are you such a klutz?" Everyone else in the hall stopped and stared.
>
> Lydia felt her face burning. Alisha and Bianca had been giving her a hard time at school for the past six weeks and she was sick and tired of it. Her first urge was to give Bianca a hard shove that would send her sprawling. At that moment, Lydia recognized it was time to apply some anger management techniques.

You can manage your angry feelings if you take charge right at the start. The anger management techniques that follow can help you keep a handle on your anger:

Recognize. The first rule for getting along with others is being able to recognize what makes you angry. Anger often occurs when you feel frustrated over something you can't control and that is important to you. The moment you feel that first flush of anger, you can make yourself stop, step back, and use self-calming techniques—before you blow your top.

Relax. To keep yourself from acting out on your anger, take several deep breaths. Then, silently and slowly, count to ten, taking a deep breath with each number. Focus on making yourself relax. The time it takes for you to slowly count to ten will give you some time to cool off and relax. This way, you can stop the fight-or-flight reaction and any impulse to be aggressive. Focusing on counting can also distract you from the person or event making you angry in the first place.

Problem solve. As you focus on your breathing, think about your options. Consider the consequences of being aggressive or violent. For example, if Lydia were to hit Bianca, what would be the outcome?

> "When angry, count ten before you speak; if very angry, a hundred."
> —Thomas Jefferson

Choosing Your Battles

Thirteen-year-old Sara decided she was spending too much time arguing and fighting with others. So she came up with an idea of how to stop. She would rate the importance of a potential argument or disagreement on a scale of 1 to 10 (with 1 being the lowest and 10 the highest priority). For example, when she was about to have an argument with her sister over whose turn it was to do the dishes, she might rank that at #1. A discussion with her parents about curfew could be #5, while being accused of cheating by her teacher would rank as a #10. Using this system, she decided to argue only when conflicts rated at #5 or above.

Sara had learned that by deciding to "choose her battles"—letting less important issues go—she had fewer conflicts with other people. She also found that in the situations where she did stand her ground, people took her more seriously.

Richard Carlson, *Don't Sweat the Small Stuff: For Teens* (2000)

There would probably be more hostility between the two girls. A physical fight could result in detention or suspension from school.

Change the environment. Give yourself time to sort things out. If you need to, remove yourself from a tense situation.

While away, use one of the following techniques to help you calm yourself. Exercising and physical

RETHINK Your Anger

The Institute for Mental Health Initiatives, based in Washington, D. C., recommends an anger management technique called RETHINK. It stands for Recognize, Empathize, Think, Hear, Integrate, Notice, and Keep.

R The moment you **recognize** you are angry, you can begin taking steps to regain control of yourself.

E When you **empathize** with the other person, you put yourself in their shoes and try to see the situation as they see it.

T With that new information you can **think** about the options you have for dealing with the situation.

H When you take the time to **hear** what the other person is saying, that gives you additional clues about why the person is acting the way he or she is acting.

I Then, you can **integrate** this information—that is, combine it with everything else you already know—in deciding what to do next.

N **Notice** means to pay attention to what it feels like to be angry.

K **Keep** refers to keeping your attention on the problem.

Put Your Anger in Writing

You might try composing a letter to the person you're angry with. It should contain everything that made you mad—don't hold anything back. You aren't actually going to mail this letter, but it should include everything you feel like saying. The next day, read it over. When you have finished, write another letter on the same topic, putting in any new thoughts you have. Then, on the following day, read your first two letters one more time before writing a third, last letter. When you finish, tear up all three letters and throw them away—along with your anger—into the trash.

activities, such as kicking a soccer ball, dancing, or jumping rope, might make you feel better. Or sing along with your favorite music. You might also call a friend and talk things over with her. Sometimes, talking about your feelings can make them less powerful. And having another person who can empathize with what you are going through can help, too.

In Lydia's case, she spun on her heel and headed off to her next class. However, she resolved that she would talk to Alisha and Bianca separately later that day. After Lydia cooled down, she arranged to meet with Bianca in the school library. Bianca seemed calmer, too. In a quiet but assertive voice, Lydia explained that she preferred being friends with Bianca but wouldn't accept being treated rudely. Although Lydia had no guarantee that her words would change Bianca's behavior, she felt better about herself for asserting herself.

Communicate. The problem won't go away if you ignore it. The best way to get someone to really listen to you is to not make that person defensive. Name-calling, trading insults, trying to tell the other person what you think she is feeling, and refusing to speak to someone will only make a bad situation worse.

CHAPTER NINE

Resolving Conflicts

What can you do if someone else is angry at you? Experts say that when someone else is yelling, you should stay calm yourself. Avoid the temptation of yelling back. Choose your words carefully, and respond in a low and even tone. Once you succeed in getting the other person to calm down, you can begin working on at least a temporary solution to the problem. However, if your attempts to get the person to calm down fail, you should leave the situation. This is especially true if you are being verbally abused or fear that the person will harm you. Before attempting to have a conversation, it is best to allow the other person to calm down.

Steps to resolve conflicts. When trying to resolve a conflict—whether with your parents, your friends, or your siblings—take some time to cool off first. Then use the following steps:

Making Choices

If handled properly, nearly every issue that could make you angry has outcomes that would improve the situation. How you choose to resolve them determines whether you've made things better. How would you handle the following situations?

1. **Your girlfriend tells you she is mad at you for not returning her call. You realize your sister never gave you the message. Would you**

    A. Not say a word about this to your sister.

    B. Ask your sister if your friend had called while you were out.

    C. Get even with your sister by not telling her the next time she misses a phone call.

2. **Your teacher gives you a C on a paper that you think deserved a B. Do you**

    A. Go home and cry.

    B. Ask the teacher to explain why you got the grade you did.

    C. Rip the paper up and tell your friends how bad the teacher is.

3. **Your classmate asks to copy your homework. Do you**

    A. Let her, even though you don't like the idea.

    B. Tell her you'd rather not, but you'd be glad to help with hers.

    C. Tell her you're not a cheater like she is.

Angry Girl? Girls Dealing With Feelings

> **4. Your friend wants to go to the movies, but you both want to see something different. Do you**
>   - **A.** Go to the movie she suggested.
>   - **B.** Tell her that you really want to see something else, and try to work it out.
>   - **C.** See the movie she suggested, but complain later about how stupid it was.
>
> In each case, the **B** answer would have put you on the right track.

- **Define the problem.** What, exactly, is the conflict about? Determine whether the fight is one single incident or a sign of a larger problem that one of you is having.

- **Talk about the problem.** Don't try to place blame on the other person. Just try to find out how the other person is feeling. Use I-messages to tell him or her what is bothering you. Listen carefully to what the other person has to say. Take responsibility for your hurtful words and actions, and apologize if you were wrong.

- **Think about solutions.** What are some things you can do to solve the problem? What can the other person do? Brainstorm a list of solutions that would resolve your conflict.

- **Evaluate the alternatives.** Come to an agreement on a solution that both of you can agree with. You may need to negotiate with each other to find a solution to your conflict that is acceptable to both of you. The word negotiate means to try to reach an agreement through discussion and compromise. When you compromise, you are giving up something important to you in exchange for reaching an agreement. For negotiation to work, you have to approach things with an open mind and be willing to listen to the other person. You can't negotiate effectively if either of you are upset or angry.
- **Follow through.** Choose a solution and carry it out. Once you've agreed on the best way to handle things, stick with your decision.

Peer mediation. Many schools have instituted programs in which two people having a conflict come to an agreement with the help of a third person. This other person acts as a mediator in their dispute. A mediator is a person who listens to both person's complaints and then tries to help them resolve their disagreement.

Peer mediation programs involve training a few students within the school in conflict resolution techniques. To help resolve conflicts, these peer mediators

> ### Think About It
> Look at past situations when you have been angry. Are there ways you could have expressed your anger differently? How did you feel about yourself afterward? How did others react? Do you think your actions resulted in positive change, negative change, or no change at all? What, if anything, would you change about your behavior going forward?

listen and ask open-ended questions. They don't give advice or take sides. And they don't have the power to determine punishments. Mediators do not come up with the solutions. Their job is to help the two students who have a conflict come to their own solutions for resolving their issues.

CHAPTER TEN

Using Your Anger

> Yesterday, Janelle learned that the money students had raised in the talent show wouldn't be given to the hurricane relief agency chosen by the student council. Mrs. Pollister, the teacher advising the council, had overruled the idea because she had never heard of the organization. Janelle was furious that Mrs. Pollister would overrule the students' decision about where they wanted their donation to go.

When you feel something is not right, anger can spur you to take action. You may feel angry because you think your decisions, beliefs, or values have been ignored or insulted. Or you may decide that a situation is wrong and you want to change it. However, if you want to be successful about bringing about change, your attitude is important.

In Janelle's case, she let some time pass in order to allow herself to calm down. Then she talked to a few other student council members and asked for their help. Together, the group sought out Mrs. Pollister and politely asked to have a talk with her. In a calm voice, Janelle explained that she knew a lot about the relief agency since her aunt worked for the organization. She gave the teacher copies of information she had found on the charity group's Web site. Then the group submitted a petition to Mrs. Pollister asking her to reconsider her decision. Janelle felt good that she stood up for herself and the other student council members.

When you feel angry because you believe someone is not treating you fairly, you need to speak up and make your voice heard. But you also want to present your case in a way that will produce positive results.

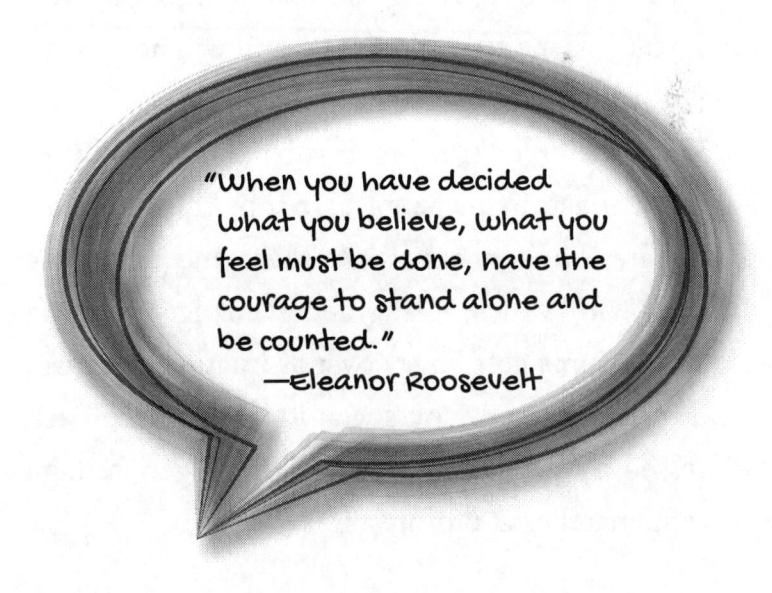

> "When you have decided what you believe, what you feel must be done, have the courage to stand alone and be counted."
> —Eleanor Roosevelt

It is not wrong to get angry. But it is wrong to express your anger in ways that hurt others or damage property.

Dealing with your angry feelings can be complicated. You want to manage and express your anger so your point of view is clearly understood. And you want the other side to be willing to listen. The best way to do that in a conflict with another individual is to be respectful. Explain your points calmly and clearly. Be assertive—not aggressive—when you stand up for what you believe to be right. Make it clear that you think you've been treated unfairly and will not accept unfair treatment.

The same holds true when you're bothered by an issue that affects many people. Do something! Make a plan, share your concerns with others, and get people to work with you to bring about change. When a group of people gets angry over a situation, they can make a difference. Many social injustices have been addressed by people expressing their anger through peaceful marches and protests.

The Woman's Right to Vote

It was the early part of the twentieth century, and one group of women in the United States was very angry. The women wanted to be able to vote in federal elections, and they couldn't. Since the 1800s, women had organized and petitioned for suffrage—the right to vote in political elections. As early as 1878, an amendment granting women suffrage had been introduced in Congress. But it never passed, despite being reintroduced again and again.

On January 10, 1917, members of the National Woman's Party (NWP) decided to take their anger over the situation to President Woodrow Wilson. On that day, suffragettes began to picket the White House, an action that women had never taken before. Protests and nonstop picketing—except on Sundays—would continue through June 1919, when Congress finally passed the amendment. Many NWP members would be arrested and jailed for their protest activities. But they continued to stand up for what they believed in.

These efforts contributed to the president calling on Congress in 1918 to pass a suffrage amendment. The 19th Amendment, which gave women the right to vote in state and federal elections, was officially ratified on August 18, 1920.

Anger Can Be Helpful When It...

1. Motivates you to accomplish a goal
2. Pushes you to solve a problem
3. Makes you see that you or someone else has not been treated fairly
4. Gives you courage and self-confidence to assert yourself or stand up for your rights
5. Pushes you to band together with other people to demand change or social justice

Good anger management skills can help you in your relationships with others both now and in the future. When you know how to express your angry feelings in a constructive way, you will feel better about yourself. And others will respect you, too.

FIND OUT MORE

Books

Greene, Ida. *Anger Management Skills for Women*. San Diego, Calif.: People Skills International, 2009.

Jantz, Gregory L., and Ann McMurray. *Every Woman's Guide to Managing Your Anger*. Grand Rapids, Mich.: Revell, 2009.

Potter-Efron, Ronald. *Rage: A Step-by-Step Guide to Overcoming Explosive Anger*. Oakland, Calif.: New Harbinger Publications, 2007.

Internet Addresses

American Psychological Association
http://www.apa.org/

TeensHealth: How Can I Deal With My Anger?
http://teenshealth.org/teen/your_mind/emotions/deal_with_anger.html

Hotlines

National Domestic Violence Hotline
1-800-799-SAFE (7233)

National Suicide Prevention Lifeline
1-800-273-TALK (8255)

INDEX

A
abuse, 25, 27, 32, 41
adrenaline, 9
adults, 30–35, 46
aggression, 9–12, 25–26
amygdala, 7–8
anger
   causes of, 7–9
   expressing, 8–12
   management, 47–52
   and motivation, 44–45, 62
   and personality, 13–18, 25–26
   physical symptoms, 4–9, 37–38
   suppressing, 36–42
anorexia nervosa, 39, 42
apologies, 21, 22
assertiveness, 15–18, 26–27, 31, 52, 60

B
body language, 33
bulimia, 39, 42
bullying, 14, 43–46

C
communication, 10–11, 18, 21, 23, 26, 33, 34–35, 52
conflict resolution, 21–22, 24, 26–27, 28–29, 53–57
cyberbullying, 44, 46

D
depression, 40–42
destructive behavior, 24, 41
divorce, 32, 39

E
eating disorders, 39–40
emotions, 5–9, 36–42
empathy, 21, 24, 50, 51
estrogen, 8
exercise, 49–51

F
fight-or-flight instinct, 5, 48
friendship, 19–24

H
health, 37–40
hormones, 8, 9
hotlines, 42

I
I-messages, 22, 23, 28–29, 55

L
learned behaviors, 18

P
parents, 18, 27, 29, 30–34, 35

passiveness, 14–15
peer mediation, 56–57
progesterone, 8
puberty, 7–8

Q
quizzes, 17, 54–55

R
relational aggression, 43
relaxation techniques, 48
respect, 26, 27, 33, 34, 45, 60, 62
RETHINK (anger management), 50

S
self-esteem, 15, 38–39
siblings, 25–29
social justice, 58–62
stress, 9, 32, 38, 41
suffrage (voting rights), 61
suicide, 41, 42
surveys, 8, 44

T
teachers, 34–35

V
venting, 26
violence, 9, 18, 25, 26, 27, 48–49

Angry Girl? Girls Dealing With Feelings

This book property of
Rector Public Library
Rector, AR 72461